DIRTSPELL

Poems by Maia Carlson

Kansas City   Missouri

Spartan Press
Kansas City, Missouri
spartanpresskc.com

Copyright © Maia Carlson, 2019
First Edition1 3 5 7 9 10 8 6 4 2
ISBN: 978-1-950380-63-3
LCCN: 2019950064

Design, edits and layout: Jason Ryberg
Cover and title page image: Jon Lee Grafton
Author photo: Riley Morsman
All rights reserved. No part of this publication may be reproduced or transmitted in any form or by any means, electronic or mechanical, including photocopying, recording or by info retrieval system, without prior written permission from the author.

Acknowledgments:

Unending thanks to Traci Brimhall, affectionately known as *Poet Mom* by many (but not nearly enough) – without her help organizing poems, giving revision suggestions, and telling me that I was a poet in the first place, this collection wouldn't even be here.

Many thanks as well to the editors of the following journals, in which some of my poems have been previously published:

"Before Abel" and "Any Winter," *Touchstone*
"Godshell," "Love Rot," and "Eclipsed by Clouds," *Z Publishing*
"Prayers to the Maternal Mover," *Rogue Agent*
"Crown Shyness," *Burmingham Poetry Review*
"Loonlight," *I-70 Review*
"Mother of Thousands," "Stone Lessons," and "In Movies No Mothers are Superheroes," *Midwest Quarterly*
"Lacunar Amnesia," *Lammergeier*

TABLE OF CONTENTS

Good morning

Summer

Dirtspell / 1

Mother of Thousands / 2

It's always cloudy this morning / 3

The Cost of Raising a Bonsai Family / 4

Stone Lessons / 5

Request of a Thunderstorm / 6

A Boneflesh Kind of Love / 7

In movies no mothers are superheroes / 8

I spent my childhood in the skins of others / 9

Three Syllables of Emotion / 10

How I Know a Fellow Gardener / 11

Love You to the Moon and Back / 12

Little Asteriscus / 13

Interdigitation / 14

Mistranslation / 16

Field Notes on the Eldingar Plant / 17

Aromantic / 18

An Elegy, an Ode, for Love / 19

Crown Shyness / 20

Eclipsed by Clouds / 21

Autumn

Poetspell / 25

Love Rot / 26

Illness Poem 1: Synesthetic Self-Dispossession / 27

Portrait of the Poet as Diptera, the True Flies / 28

Lacunar Amnesia / 30

Anxiety / 31

Illness Poem 2: Anthophila Crystallization / 32

La Fin du Monde / 33

Loonlight / 34

I don't want to be told my scars make me beautiful / 35

Cinderbrand Girls / 37

Illness poem 3: Glacial Masturbation Syndrome / 38

Bestiary of the Poet / 39

Self-possession / 41

Predator / 42

Shibari / 44

Illness Poem 4: Multifaunal Identity Disorder / 45

Translating the Dead / 46

A Skeleton in Everything / 47

A Funeral / 48

I hold my death here / 49

Winter

Wingspell / 53

Family Graves / 54

I Dreamt I Mourned for Whale Bones / 55

An ode to the bagpipe, which is still classified as a weapon of war and therefore not allowed in churches / 56

You open your house to me / 57

How to Know Death / 58

Postpartum / 59

Dislocated Sadness / 60

Numb / 61

Any time I try to write a poem / 62

Before Abel / 64

I was going to call this *necrophilia* / 67

The Four Beasts of Tribulation / 70

We Skin Ourselves Daily / 71

Field Notes on the Splinterbone Tree / 72

Dear Phoenix / 73

Chiaroscuro of Your Dark / 76

No one / 78

Any Winter / 79

Spring

Dayspell / 83

Honey for Bones / 84

Brave / 85

Asexuality / 86

Request of a Tsunami / 89

After five years of nurture and heartache,
 the Hoya bloomed / 90

The Happiness of the Poet / 92

Prayers to the Maternal Mover / 93

Chats in a Rain Garden / 96

The Greatest Smile / 97

Boy, when you're outside during a milk moon / 99

Virago / 100

The New Sacrament / 101

Mirror / 102

Sing, sing, cursor mundi / 103

Happiness in Green / 104

Prayer for a Long Union / 105

Daughtermoth, become a queen / 106

Good Morning

I can feel
the excitement like first snow
beneath my skin, testing new notes
beneath raised hair follicles, like a song
that I know I'll have to sing a few times in tandem
with the cardinals before the daughterless tune will know
    my throat and take
up residence like the golden taste of buttered toast
or the rosy glimmer of dawn's lance
through an amaryllis bloom.

Summer

Dirtspell

My father was once told that he had spirits watching over him, a triad of souls. That explains perhaps how a sixty-five-year-old man can still referee soccer, touch his toes, teach his children how to fall. My mother was told by the same fortuneteller that she'd marry the man she came with – which was true, but which also meant my mother had to find her magic with her hands. So while my father reminds me daily of the miracles we cannot explain, my mother buries both our hands in the roots of her hydrangea, showing me how the simple application of wood ash, lime, or phosphorus will transform the dull green blooms she calls a *lifeless limb color* into the bright pink of baby-palms, toothless gums, healthy flesh.

Mother of Thousands

but not of yourself, take
your crown of green with its soft
living edges, and dash it
upon the ground like you're scattering
a rainfall. Take your earthen hands
and grip your own roots
as if to pull them away from the core
of all you've grown up in.
There's only dirt here, but
it's fed you; only stone,
but it's anchored you.
You must threaten change,
and make your tethers tremble,
from seed to seed unto
the edges of your world.

it's always cloudy this morning

the storm is like a throat
of lions
to cubs   singing
         a continuous thunder of heritage
rasping out purrs   between tongues of
you don't exist   until lightning strikes
        you're only what the light touches, simba
you can only sit in air as warm as a skin
and hold in the blackness like a breath
        and wait   to live longer two seconds
knowing that the molecules of the world
are changed in that light petrichor made
        of a sound that won't hit you
until three heartbeats
remind you of the rib   adam supposedly gave
you
        but which feels like the jawbone
scribbled redly into samson's will
as your chest vibrates with a sort of punctuated violence
        that you can no more hold safely
than the bellied clouds can hold
their 1.1 million pounds of weight
without golden groaning

The Cost of Raising a Bonsai Family

Don't raise children like bonsais, my mother quotes another mother while we pull Queen Anne's Lace from the garden. *The art of bonsai is a practice in torture.* I mother and smother the leaves of weeds and imagine their stalks bent and contorted as we talk. My father tries to kill stray mulberry trees every spring, as they crawl up out of the ground like Lazarus branches. Their stalks linger after the cutting, thumb-thick and crooked, and I fancy them bonsais without the work. You don't have to pay for hacksawed mulberry stumps. Gnarled weeping willow bonsai on Etsy: $45, plus shipping that may or may not deliver your tree alive. Ficus bonsai with bared roots like bulbous, naked futility figures at Walmart: $25, plus the gas to drive there and the soul-deep disappointment of every Walmart greeter. Digging wayward mulberry saplings from beneath the old spruce tree in the spring, after my father beheaded them in the fall: incalculable. Just the cost of imprinted dirt beneath my fingernails, and waxed spruce needles biting my knees as I kneel and dig. Find the taproot. Hold the surviving mulberry leaves back with grime-riddled hands. Feel their hopeful green veins kiss the dirt-lined lifeline down my palm as I misuse my mother's second-best cutlery for digging, favoring the dexterous spoon over the brutal spade. Contort myself to dodge the low-hanging spruce branches above and dig like the stubborn mulberry root, down to the priceless world below.

Stone Lessons

Things the opal taught me: that so long as you can let a bit of light inside of you, you'll see something stunning, even if it's crackling stormlight through a stab-wound, and the only beauty you see is your own soul.

Things the garnet taught me: that the bloody red center of you isn't something to be ashamed of, even if it glints like a tiger's growl, even if it's tinted dark by the proximity to your heart. You can look like gore but still be strong.

Things the labradorite taught me: that you must capture inside of you the most gorgeous things that you see, but hold them always to the surface of your skin, like a tattoo from the inside out, like a peacock-colored stain.

Things the obsidian taught me: that we can be impressive even when we are raw, even when we are unmade, our veins splayed like knife-blades, our eyes dark yet clear, the flaws shattered out of us. You can look at an enemy and warn *I break in dangerous ways.*

Things the onyx taught me: that darkness has no depth that we do not give it.

Request of a Thunderstorm

Beautiful storm, speak in tongues
so loud that you set my teeth deeper in my jaw
and feed me a clean, white anger
until I don't know hunger anymore—
a kind of fury that we sad bags of lonely water
don't have anywhere in our vocal chords or the birdcage
of our chest—no word
for that hot, cleansing fire
that isn't already bright with the kind of red Job found
beneath his fingernails from scratching at his own
sense of having been wronged.
Beautiful storm, give me a word for 'hatred'
that doesn't hurt this small vessel that speaks it,
for such a present would be as colossal as the eye of a storm
in the palm of my hands—so that I may say
I don't have to forgive you
and taste only water on my tongue
and feel clean.

A Boneflesh Kind of Love

My mother's hands peel the dirt back from its backbone of earth. Her gloves are discarded, lost one at a time in the pathway from plant to pot, potting soil to seed, plant bed to plant bed. She guides my hand away when I try to sink the New Guinea Impatiens into the dirt beside the discordant trestles of variegated Vinca vine. She speaks like it's obvious, like it's bone-to-flesh: *No. Impatiens love shade. This pot is for sun.* We settle *Apocynaceae* into the cool dark instead, its roots like fingers reaching gratefully for the clasp of another loamed hand.

In movies no mothers are superheroes

but I learned today in a waking
        dream that for some, the only path
to heroics is through a monstrous birth, women
ejecting from themselves
        something both ugly and loved, and sometimes
you have to kill that thing, because sometimes
we don't choose it, sometimes,
        that clot of gruesomeness is sewn in us
by other hands, a red blessing, a quote-unquote-
gift the no one ever believes
        they'd give a woman, because mothers
never make superheroes, mothers
die to make way for superheroes. But
        when I sleep I dream
of standing naked beneath a Healing Tree, and I feed
its re-broken-grown-back-ugly roots with incarnadined wetness
        down my thighs and tell her that
she doesn't have to give so much.

I spent my childhood playing in the skins
of others

sitting still for the length of time it took to lattice together
the skeleton of another being, a bonehouse carefully
crafted in my mind so I could step into it. I'd hold
myself very still, eyes closed, all the better to straighten
out threaded thoughts. Inhale and the loom shivered,
the creels stirred; exhale and the shuttle danced like a
boat across the tautened warp. Recess was for wedging
myself halfway down the tunnel slide, so that I could
hear the voices of other children but still concentrate
on the construct in my head, as I built the rich laughter
necessary for a woman who slays dragons. I still make
skins for myself, finding work meetings instead of
playground equipment, and my shuttle still dances
and weaves all the same, while I hum at a pitch below
hearing: *Skin and bone, skein and loom, skin and bone,
skein and loom.*

Three Syllables of Emotion

As we sit in a brindled light and talk about darkness, my poet-mother describes emotions as an ocean, an arms'-width wide and a soul's-throw deep. She describes to me the plunge necessary to dredge the depths, to survive the pressure changes when you move from happiness to hurt, from sorrow to surface, and the bends that occur when you claw too fast back to happiness. *Emotions are something to learn how to drown in,* she says as a cloud passes and halves the light, *to inhale until you grow gills or your heart stops.* As we dab hot glue on chopsticks and call them magic wands, my art-sister describes emotions as roots, tendrils that she casts out towards the worthy. She says that she feels deeply for those who deserve it, burrowing deep into the earth of her mind and feeling each shiver of their connection, like she's growing into them. Others, she severs, and through the abrogated root feels nothing for those who have hurt her once. The wand sizzles as the nozzle of the hot glue gun presses too close, singing the magic into the wood. *Emotions are bonsai branches to be tended tenderly or broken bitterly,* she says. To me, emotions are a wolf, leashed and muzzled by logic. I see its fur, black and boiling. The night I learned my friend had been abused, its eyes peridot. Like the pear I cradled in my hand while a farm dog attacked my littlest sister. Everything light, brindled and singed.

How I Know a Fellow Gardener

Your body still work-warm
and peat-moss soft
and your heart open like
a dogwood bloom
given two years to grow
its roots down before
opening its crown up

Your love spoken
in fifty-dollars worth of orchids
and five split irises sunk
into richer earth

Your closeness
like redbud petals
suckled close and pink
to the bark

Love You to the Moon and Back

I lived   I loved
I loomed   I   –consumed–
a white-jawed wolf to
wolf it down
that cream-clotted throat   a coated moat
a river of brindled light
to fight the journey of the jaw   to the belly   to the soul
like coal it sits   in fits and   spits a
chokecherry   ire   an excised fire

oh, you clay-baby soul, you don't know
          the dogstar yet   crushing your quiet like
chokecherries and Carthage
          like Aningan loved Malinas
                    like Tulok crushed into stars across the matte
          black sky. Cry when you stare up
                    bare up your throat like Sirius,

          until you walk outside when the mint it rotting
                    and the moon hangs herself like the world's
     dewclaw
                         because only a wolf with one blind
     eye knows both
the wonder   and   the dark.

Little Asteriscus

remember, you are a denotation of great things, a tiny furled light with as much brightness as sharp edges, and he was like the rubber boa, who teases the mother mouse with the false head of his fat tail, letting her scar only his farthest reaches while he gulps down mouselings one by one, into the dark night of his throat. But remember, Little Asteriscus, the deeper and darker you go, the brighter and more defended you become, if you only pause to unfurl your pearl-dust hands.

Interdigitation

I love a body for its hands, the smooth conviction of
language from carpels to metacarpals, nothing lost in
translation, as articulated as a cat's spine. I love the lies
and truths interlaced in eleven married bones, and how
I can say *I love you* or *I hate you* just by holding your throat.

While the open hand disillusions the palmed coin, or
reveals the crushed bloom, the closed fist can reveal scars
selling secrets upon the knuckles, as candid as the cuts that
birthed them. I love how hands balance the imperfect and
the perfect like blind Lady Justice, whose rules don't apply

in nature, where the barn owl is born with imbalanced
ears. Each skull is deformed with one ear higher than the
other, perfectly broken like a mute hand yet more capable
of hearing the sighs of mice than any machine. I love hands,
but the mouth's words I distrust as I distrust rats, who can

collapse their ribcages and lead their supple bodies
through any hole their heads can fit. Words, like rats,
will go anywhere they please and even the bones can't be
trusted. And I don't love eyes because they're windows,
gaping holes in the face to the ugly truth of souls, because

there is such a thing as too much truth, the nudity of self like a skinned body, fleshed with nothing but too much clarity and not enough meat to hide in. The eyes crinkle, smile-lines like nets cast by the grinning mouth to catch truths that escape like fish jumping from their bowl, floundering while the mouth lies, bracketed by dimples like a rodent's slim hipbones.

Mistranslation

when i said *i love you* i meant hummingbird feet clenched on
branches shitting over the side while wetting their beaks with
a mulberry squish stainso fragile you could cry but you heard

dopamine norepinephrine adrenaline and serotonin like a well-
bred craziness on my breath and you cracked open the birds'
bones looking for a place to bury yourself when i said *goodbye*

i meant whale bones at the bottom of an ocean worms across
and within it hagfish and sharks with blind eyes like mirrors
the only feast they've had in lifetimes but you heard

kingfishers diving into deep lakes and the cobalt swallowing
them all black and blue with a spearing beak no promise of
return no sky in your palms

Field Notes on the Eldingar Plant

Small and fragile
never taller than a hawk's curved beak
leaves folded like scales   tight-fisted   asks for nothing

Thunderheads roll in, palisades of white and gun-metal grey
crowding from one branch of the sky to another
each armed strike of lightning cracks N_2 into something
    plants can feed on
leaves flex and extend   afraid to take anything but
   that which is given most brutally electrically

Stalk a whimsied fang
fiddlehead curve
Helix pomata beneath the reaching leaves
photosynthesizes only in the thunderous dark

Aromantic

love is an affliction
of the *honeymoon phase*
cut short, my body draining
of dopamine and norepinephrine

like an ocean escaping through
a keyhole, leaving behind all
of the fascination of the vast sea
floor with octopi overturned, suckers grasping,

urchins with their bodies spearing
the new blue of the sky and my body
filled with the fresh air I hadn't known
to miss and my mouth shaping the words

Before now the world was drowning,
and I'll stroke your gills, my own
smooth, unblemished neck and inhale
great lungfulls of air from my cupped palms.

Nose to my own skin, thinking
But this one smells like the sun

An Elegy, an Ode, for Love

I love you like the owl takes in gifts. She's silent, grateful, and chokes down all of the mice and leverets you feed her, until I can feel the uncomfortable prickling of foreign ribs down my gullet. Undigested, she coughs up what she can't keep, and it's more than you expect, just like you can't understand how I transmogrified your love so artlessly.

I love you like the Thylacine speaks. She's soft, guttural, so hard to hear that you try to find easy meaning in the stripes down her back, until I can feel the deaf, lost prodding of your fingertips on my spine, digging for a dead language. Marsupial, she coaxes the things she loves up inside of her, but her pouch is deep and backwards, and I doubt you'll ever find it.

I cannot love you like the Wendigo, whose hunger would swallow you whole and whose appetite grows with every kiss, every jawing, every internecine war of saliva and teeth. He's born of desperation, of a desire for one body within another, but there's no famine in me; no howl at my core.

Crown Shyness

In the love poem I cannot write, I talk about orchids, and air roots, and the way young bark bends beneath wire. I tell you I'm the *Phalaenopsis*, and how it feels like putting me in a casket in the ground when you plant me like any other flower – my roots need air, not the coffin-crush of earth. I say I'll promise to give your leaves enough sun in return. In the break-up poem I cannot write, I compose unrhymed lines about how I make bonsais from weeds instead of buying them, because I'm cheap, but I end up letting my weeds grow because I can't stand to cripple them how I want to. People say bonsais are beautiful only after they've wrapped them in wire for years. In the apology poem I cannot write, you stand at the heart of a forest and look up. It's like looking at a dried up lake: the surface above riddled with cracks, making each tree's leafy head into an island. They're crackling with perfect green life, but the arms of one tree refuse to touch the hands of another.

Eclipsed by Clouds

Totality
was like an umbilical cord
being severed, and like birth,
you can never go back.

I remembered
the post-womb fear
even as the clouds billowed
and closed
their ashen eyes above me.
I, the husband, was

shut out of the birthing room,
but I could sense, like a
godly dislocation, something being
cut as the unborn darkness fell.

Autumn

Poetspell

One eye of the owl not for wisdom but for
the eerie twist of their head, the novel angle
of vision, a neck rotated past breaking
Two tusks of the Babirusa pig, which must only be
harvested after they have grown and angled
and pierced the skull of their keeper,
spilling forth the sly, earthen knowledge
of all swine, mixing it with self-destruction
Three claws of the Hoatzin bird, not
from the foot but by the chick's wing,
is origins remembered in three fingers
which you will take before they lose them
at adulthood – don't lose them,
in your own adulthood.
Grind together in a mortar and pestle
made all of fine obsidian, its edges
all hidden away in its core, like words polished
from lacerating to river-water smooth.
Mix with milk and honey as the fey do,
but do not drink, for poets do not need smears
upon their tongues. Dig in with your fingers
instead, so that the world can leave itself
beneath your fingernails.

Love Rot

I'll follow you like the raven follows the wolf between kills. I don't need you, but I want you. I'll love you like the cuckoo-bird loves the warbler, betrayal in every crack of the egg I beg you to cherish. My favorite color is the incongruous coral of turtledove feet, picked out against the background of asphalt and fallen, crushed mulberries. I see the colors in you; hearts are mulberries, lips are coral. My garnet wedding ring looks like a gobbet of blood set in stone, a gift from the corpse to the crow.

Illness Poems 1: Synesthetic Self-Dispossession

When you haven't heard the rainsound in too long and
a mermaid you never knew wakes up in your soul only
to paint the inside of your chest with the word *cage* and
scream the color blue across the backs of your eyes where
you cannot see it. Your body has sunk out on itself, buckled
until you're gazing out through the stoma of an orchid leaf,
wandering about the glass that keeps you in and keeps the
soaked moth out. Its wings are crying, each a heartbeat.

Portrait of the Poet as *Diptera*, the True Flies

What meaning is within
the body, curled within
the small, eroded
wings the pencil-
shaving legs, the

Dance Fly, of the Family *Empididae*
—sounds like "empty-all-day"—
as he dances on pencil-
shaving legs, what's
in the body? What's
gone from the body,

Robber fly, of the Family *Asilidae*
—sounds like a stereotype—a
gangster family
hoarded up in lore. What
can we take and keep? What
is mercurial and gripless
to small, haired feet? What
do we fight for, tooth and
proboscal mouth, making us a

Soldier fly, of the family *Stratiomydae*,
—sounds like an order—to insects

shallow in their graves yet
deep within their
carapaces, deep within their
names. What is in the earthen holes
we dig ourselves, what
graven images has the world
saddled us with? Are we within
our names?

Lacunar Amnesia

The book, the one where I learn about the Castrati, where the rat of my mind starts turning, sits on the highest shelf where I wait for my mother's cataract surgery, the blue book with the gold leaf – *Cry to Heaven* – but spiders castrate, too, males dragging off their sexual organs half or in whole, and scientists study it like ants might study the toenails of gods while my father asks how long the surgery will take and I stroke the well-loved spine and think how it reminds me of reindeer eyes – the dayless dark of the Arctic winter turning them from gold to blue – *The tapetum lucidum is blue,* I read, researching my mother's eyes, because reindeer get glaucoma, too, *in winter, whereas the eyeshine of most mammals is always gold* like when my mother's eyes began failing, so that she'd see three moons moaning down at her where I saw one, and my professor pulled out a poor stuffed rat of a thing and pronounced, *The flying squirrel. Call it glaucomys on tests – Latin for silver mouse,* and I wonder if flying squirrels get glaucoma and flew towards three moons, or if glaucoma is a silver disease, or if, like the pages in an old book, their memories are tied together by little stubborn strings that we can't see. My mother comes out of surgery like nothing had ever happened.

Anxiety

1. My body feels like a glass vase,
like a transient space, a skin
I label *home*

2. I keep my worries in a well
—too shallow—
in the dark of my mind;
a silo for rottenness

3. The dogtoothed itch hides
at the tip of each finger to pick at—
in scabs
to worry open.
One day I hope
to give this sliver
to a god that never sleeps.

4. Buried beneath the willow,
beneath the well, in the core of an apple
it will grow
a crooked, protective tree
with spined, white branches
that I'll live in
and walk among the thorns like birds do.

Illness Poem 2: Anthophila Crystallization

When you feel like a meatsuit full of heartbeats but want to sink into a bath of tourmaline and amber, brecciated jasper for a heartstone. Your eyes are set on the little white flowers of the snowflaked obsidian but you won't waste honey on tea.

La Fin du Monde

My mother taught me how to smell the earth quickening, the smell of rising sap like the sweetness of Canadian honey that her mother always brought out in spring – and she taught me how the last place to rain is always under the trees, in big, fat, kissing drops. My father taught me that three steps back and one to the left is always in a person's blind spot, and how to choose branches to cut by where they rub each other raw. When we returned to Canada for my grandfather's funeral, we hid at our cabin and broke branches on the path to the lake, so that the three of us could stand there in the rain that fell like sheets. We all understood, as storm ebbed and rose, that the world stopped where the curtain of rain began. We trusted – we had to – that our thoughts would start again on the other side.

Loonlight

In the lake my brother did not drown in, the loon knows that his mate's bones are built to sink and not to fly, so while the thrush and the meadowlark serenade their lovers with promises of yellow flowers and buttercup hours, the loon howls across the lake, low and longing, high and haunting. Her body is speckled like cold stars on a moonless night, and she cries – he knows these things about her, so he sings to her, *I'll bring you bones and thrones, and everything else you could wish for.* And if she likes it, they sink like stones, their feathers slicked back like my brother's hair for a wedding, a funeral.

I don't want to be told that my scars
make me beautiful

We bleed the cut-points
because the world says *Glorify the scars, why
waste your time on healing?* I walk

every day past a redbud tree and today
a young man with shears cut away
the suckers from the dark trunk, the little branches

that grew from her nooks and crannies
and slowly bled her dry with their loving,
and although the rest of her canopy

was leafy and green, three days later
she sprouted little purple buds
frantically around the places

where the suckers had been, like mouths
shouting *There is nothing wrong here! Nothing
lost! I'm grateful for the wound.*

I call my biggest scars
my shadow, sometimes going before me,
sometimes after. Don't tell me

that my pain deserves
a better name, nor a better place
than beneath my feet. The brown earth

can hold my scars. They're
not yours.

Cinderbrand Girls

You see eye-
shadow in the shade
of your own desires
and dark hollow places
to fill up.
Damsel and dragon
all in one, to save and destroy,
stroke by stroke. Street corners
with bodies leaned up against them.
So regrettable. But
we don't follow
our dreams; we hunt coals
to breathe life into them
like the gods used to.
We're sooty, we're
sulfurous flames
tinged the color of minerals
and scorch earth.
Our lips aren't bitten; they're a
bite me red, and
we're covered in
the afterbirth of stars;
we're ugly with it.
We're three layers of paint
with a phoenix underneath.

Illness Poem 3: Glacial Masturbation Syndrome

When you can't remember when you weren't warm honey in a new skin, squeeze your core to milk it. You'll know it by the smell of foxes, your nose buried in her nape, her body a velvet shiver in your arms. Nobody gave you this so you can swallow all your *thank yous,* let them harden into a solitary godstone at the level of your iliac, frost it with the sweetness of slow blinks, half breaths, and veins that swell with nepenthes.

Bestiary of the Poet

I've stepped into the dark to meet with myself
and I've come away just empty
enough to fill with little bits of
alular feathers and bastard wings,
dismantled bits of catbone
and a thread of dogsteel
to bind it all together.

I've trundled eight long legs
through a field of hellebore and redvein
just to feel the little mortal whisper
of petals lipped against my
cuttlebone skin
where the blood is closest
to the outside world.

I've practiced a minkish love
in which I've sunk teeth into hearts
bigger than mine and
fingermapped my way into other henhouses,
between other thighs, under
other breastbones
where cinderbranded scars
take the shape of butterflies.

I've stepped into the dark to meet with myself
and I've come away whole
enough to be like the lungs of the earth,
brittlebranched
—breathe in—

Self-possession

My friend learned her spirit animal
was a swan and said she didn't feel
like it, so I told her that swans
break bones with their wedding-gown-white
wings and hold loyalty like a sorrow-
song until death.

I told myself that my spirit animal
was an opal stone, something bright
and living within a stone shell, taking
everything in with a flamed tongue
of polished greed.

I told another friend, don't always feed
the falcon in your soul.
Let her come to you, open-beaked;
keep her fast,
keep her hungry.

Predator

Barracuda dangerous, your head beneath a shattered crown.
It hits me somewhere uncracked inside my chest that you're a
glove of bullet ants that some young boys stick their hands into
to prove that they've become men through pain.

Hands a gift upon the body, deposing gods in the dark is what
you do, a song you sing from somewhere iron-kind and shrike-
like in your core.

You nestle up behind me and slide a hand beneath my ribcage
until your fist becomes my heart, knuckled and sealed, like the
burrowed nest of the bone-house wasp, where she cradles and
keeps what she loves.

I understand the python now, how it gapes wide
kisses to the depths of its soul, and
unhinges its jaw to deepthroat the things it most adores.
To you that is love, as your soul knows it
as your mouth shows it, when I make gods of myself—
foolishly, and you depose me in the dark.

The hook you keep nestled under your tongue is a glory
of god and of war, and you don't distinguish between the two.
Curled up against your breast, I see in you
the shrike, and how possessively and meticulously it spines
prey upon the barbed-wire fence.

Your chest could crack open and eat me, the cinder-soft
center of you taking all that makes me a conqueror
and burn it alive. You've grown yourself
nine tales and named yourself my itinerant god
and like the bone-house wasp you mingle carnage with love.

Barn owl beautiful, and iron-kind your love.
It strikes me, somewhere fleshy and giving
that when you press your fingers to my tongue you could as easily
unhinge your jaw and swallow me whole, and that would still be
love as your predator-soul knows it.

Shibari

I'm a hot breath I'm
two ropes drawn down
between your thighs   hemp   caress
skin raised   abrasioned   like a rose
I'm that fold in the rope called
the bite all twisted close
to a bent thigh   folded   closed
like a wing a wing   you don't need it angel
you don't need anything
that I haven't given you   I'm
a coil tightly woven between the bird bones
of your ankles   draw you up
off the ground in a nest of knots
I'm a tight hand binding the ropes
up tighter   higher   trust me
more than gravity and flesh and pain
give me that tiny sigh that comes
from the pocket behind your heart
give me what sex won't give you give
the release of hands curled loose
around your own elbows   against your back
ropes a kiss   skin remembers the patterns
crisscrosses of blush-red and little
bruises where the knots rested

Illness Poem 4: Multifaunal Identity Disorder

When you feel like Strobilanthes. Persian shield plant, sand in my teeth, roots veining out from my heels. I fear that I'll die before the frosts come, flowers still curled like pearled tumors beneath my fingernails. When you feel like Styrax. Weeping Japanese snowbell, thoughts hung in petals. They say my rounded white crown is deciduous, and that the scars in my bark grow attractive in winter. When you feel like Adenium. Desert rose plant, the Sabi start, toxins for coating arrowheads. Cut me and I'll grow fat on it.

Translating the Dead

My father brought home a dead owl once, like a cat proud of its mouse. We were both immune to that abattoir feel because death means less to a farmer's son, a doctor's daughter who dissected invertebrates in a lab. The owl's busted eye and blood-ruffled throat said, *Illegal shooting,* and we felt like criminal investigators walking the path of the bullet with our eyes and fingers. The owl's remaining eye glared as golden as a dragon's whole hoard, and its tufted head alluring as a hot stove to a child's touch. *Tufts are just for show,* I told my father, as we touched what we've only seen in books. It was as downy as blown smoke and scraped whispers free against the pads of my fingers. *The real ears are a treasure.* And my father watched as I put my science to the use of my hands, and reached forward to stroke the rim of feathers beside the one remaining gold—God, so gold—eye, a face-plate of feathers that looks like a shield, or a dinner plate. I've never seen science come so alive before as on a dead bird when I parted the feathers at the edge of that useless downy shield to reveal the ear slit gaping, pink, full of alien whorls like something artistic or dissected. *I've never seen anything so drop-dead gorgeous,* I remember saying, thinking: the eye of the basilisk, a wonder no one gets to look at twice.

A Skeleton in Everything

There's a skeleton in everything, a musculature for every bone, a thought articulated like a cat's spine buried beneath your tongue before it moves. That artist's masterpiece, a horse thundering beneath a maelstrom sky, each slick sable stroke of oil paint, brushed over what bones an artist sees beneath, arched calcifications driven like invisible needles through the page. We build as we sketch. A brush-stroke skinning blood and sinew across parchment whiteness, bone whiteness. The architect looks and sees the bones of an old building sinking like a New Orleans mausoleum into the earth. He thinks of resurrection. Can he raise and polish that paint-chipped ribcage? Reshape those snarled, gnarled, arthritic metatarsals? Or should he just bust it off at the femurs and play god, create it anew. Admit it, we are all Frankenstein, because there's a skeleton in everything and our hands ache to show that it lives.

A Funeral

Inside looks like
the ribcage of the Ark
if God gutted and overturned it,
made an urn
and spilled its ashes in long,
bone-slick pews. The ashes
in their burnt shades
stand uncertainly,
unsure what mourning looks like,
mouths clogged with coffin-
songs like damned holy instruments
before a coffin as white as a femur
beneath a sword of Damocles,
weighty and bladed,
molded into a cross.

I hold my death here

in the ribboned vessels
behind my sternum.
It hibernates and brushes
pale lashes
against my diaphragm
as it blinks. I carry it,
unborn, like a mother;
Meat and bones but no breath.
      Trace the ribs. Try to find a way in.
it smells like wet leaves
feels like shivered, shed skin.
I can see it like a third eye
pinned open beneath my Solar Plexus.
So I hide it like a dried cocoon
with the butterfly still in it.
      Crack the sternum. It's a doorway.

Winter

Wingspell

My grandmother's citrine wings fold unchastely against the grill of my car. I never told her how I took comfort in the velvet-soft fragility of her cheek when she leaned in to kiss me, but I don't know how to say it now to those buckled forewings and crooked spindles of legs. I can stroke the powder-downed edge of a hindwing, but no one told me how to touch a lost loved one. When I walk away, I spot a black swallowtail sunning itself on the sidewalk. Does it know another soul-carrier is dead, its carapace bruised across an automotive net? When I approach, the soul fans itself slowly, only taking off when my shadow crosses it.

Family Graves

There's an inheritance in the body. I'm wearing the skin my mother shed for me, intact right down to the translucent eye-caps, which grow clearer every time I press my eyes up behind them. I'm constantly adjusting the bones my father unburied for me when he dug into worn muscles with wide, skilled hands. The ribs had already learned – caved inside another body – how to hug lungs and heart together beneath their studied span. Measuring them for me was easy, my father said. Together it fits well. It feels whole. I can almost ignore the zippered steps of the spinal cord, the loose stitching at the eyelashes. I go to sleep in the bones of my father and wake to the flesh of my mother. Their graves are comfortable. Loving. When aunts declare, *You look just like your mother,* and uncles chime, *You remind me of your father,* I preen, heart-deep.

I Dreamt I Mourned for Whale Bones

It's a family tradition to call home and speak
of deaths like casting stones across northern lakes
too green to be unclouded.
When my mother calls home to tell me of
three disasters in childbirth,
they are none of them related.
Our family is safe in glass houses
while we speak drops in an ocean about how
the shells rock to the rhythm of the tide
and the tide rocks
to the rhythm of past whale-song;
our mouths test the words
let me test the fullness of your womb
while we forget all names of loss
that are not our own.

An ode to the bagpipe, which is still classified
as a weapon of war and therefore not allowed
in churches

The dead take up
as much space as an ocean and

church roofs look like vaulting ribs
upturned, dry-heaved, bone-caged.

They do not know how to speak
and hold silence instead of a heart

but then the bagpipes start warming
up like a storm's first inhale

they break the quiet to
make room for themselves; the chanters

mesh into triple-harmonics, three lungs
clearing three throats, *I am here you am here*

we are here; a forewarning before
they cry out with a holy wildness

dug from the deep peat of the moors
and depressed bellows, lungs and heart

in one, and a loan moan
comes from a throat that has sobbed before

You open your house to me

though I give you neither bread nor
bone nor the pleasure of even one breath
from the hollow of my mouth. I am thing thing
you invited in without threat or warning, the cold
locked away beyond the sacred maw of your threshold.
I know the logs on the hearth are for me, the honey and
cream shared freely, until I can taste the history of giving
    again on my tongue.
You open your house to me like it is our ribs, and you'd
    part them
so that I could find a forever-place within the lovely
    scaffolding
beyond; so that I could fall asleep to the unhurried rhythm
of you. In return, sweet being, I swear it, this house
will have all the protection of summoned spirit
within it. For they did not tell you, but
when you let a monster in,
something it grows
warm.

How to Know Death

I know that butterflies
are the souls of the dead
because even when one beats
powder-blue, swallowed-tailed, painted-lady
fists against my door
it would be wrong to invite them in.

The oldest living tiger
was Machli, the Crocodile Killer,
with stripes down her back
and blood on her face. At her death
her body said *I broke my teeth
on the backs of monsters.*

Postpartum

~~Don't tell~~ the story about
the newly ~~emptied~~ mother, child
in her arms ~~but fled from the geode~~
~~of her womb, don't~~ Tell the story
about how birth is about the opening
of ~~a grave All mother's must carry~~
two hearts over a sea of roses ~~of Jericho~~
~~Because I was told that~~ At a birthing,
all mothers' ~~graves are laid open and sit~~
~~yawning for 40 days because they~~
tell a story about ~~how easy it is~~
~~to watch~~ the bloom
~~while the roots are dying~~

Dislocated Sadness

My mother named all of the plants in the church after dead people, so I stare up through Birdy Lee's cupped-hand leaves and try to find her omnipresent smile in the fronds. Crying beneath the prayer-plant feels like petrichor. I trace the vivid veins and stems back, to find the sadness. My thoughts hinge on the edges of the terracotta pot and refuse to tumble own into the grave-dirt, where Birdy Lee's wise-woman roots are waiting. My mother should have named it Susanna, after the organist whose son died too young. That plant would have known how to explain my tears to me.

Numb

We leave a hole behind when we take the pain away, and think the emptiness is deadlier than the hurt we're missing. Starving wolves, we all circle back to the wounds that bleed us, dig at the sinews to know the scream is ours. Bastard demigods, we chain our leviathans in glass bowls starve them on fish flakes until they'll eat silver needles, because we expect them to solve the problem by stitching themselves closed. I once read that *Opera is when a guy gets stabbed in the back and instead of bleeding he sings*. But canaries in our coalmines herald devastation in the prettiest of ways. They know we've nothing to crawl back into but the grave-like cave we've excavated, but we keep digging, because we think each shovel-shaped scar will make us more whole. Instead, we've only the razor-dark hole; we've expelled the noise, the howl, the holiness, the heartsblood.

Any time I try to write a poem

I have a dead god in my head. A dormant divinity, he died
and slipped his leash and came home to me cold
as any winter. Found my altars empty.
Crow-beggar,
glossy feathers traded for scraps.
Beneath the xyresic cloak of god-hood
scraped raw,
harsh as any Atlas shouldering the stars.
Such a bladed, star-sharp soul.
Silk-steel,
maelstrom eyes
bundled up on the other side of madness
where dreams and old gods couple.
He curls like a Cat *Sith* on a crippled throne.
Sleeping Oberon for my teething thoughts.
Awake, he's a new religion,
and he blasphemes
shamelessly as he goes. He smiles
bloody and he kisses sharp.
Black chrysanthemum smile,
so fearsome-sweet and fire-frail
that you'll never know the Mona Lisas
he's given it to before.

But his bared teeth
like any nest-full of knives, trade
warmongering for worship
like precise cuts, prayer for bloody
beautiful prayer.
A divine currency,
a penny for my thoughts.

Before Abel

I was born at the crossing of two bones
which is like the crossing of
two words, who have to break
each other
a little
just to fit.
Words like shatterglass and thunderkite,
cinderglass and bitterbite.

I was born at the crossing of two bones:
jawbone and
fangbone.
Two beasts met with irreconcilable differences, I suppose.
Isn't that just the way of things?
With an ashdown snow
and a bleakblown wind,
an old woman with pebbles
for eyes and stretched hide
for a face
saw fangbone and jawbone locked,
two corpses
cuddled in the ashdown snow.
I've seen Irish Elk, with their antlers thus enmeshed,
snugged up tight like lovers
with their hands in each other's ribcages.

Is a religion ever born
of anything less?

I was born at the crossing of two bones
as an Ice-age woman picked up two bare-boned skulls
and saw me
in four glaring eye-sockets.
My flesh-coat gone but a bone-house was enough,
enough for her to see
whatever makes mankind
believe.
I breathed in belief through twin bleached nasal passages.

I've been born a thousand times before.
From first real sin—
of one brother crossing another
unto death; vengeance is messy
and long-lasting—
to the raising of the jawbone of an ass
to the divinity an old woman saw in kissing skulls,
to wars that stretched across nations.
Alexander was Great—
great for a breakbone, crushstone god like me.
I've never been born so alive as in the battle-
fields he sowed me in.

Immortal doesn't mean living forever, perhaps.
Perhaps.

Perhaps it means being reborn again
every time someone has a bone to pick with another.
You remember Cain
but I remember Abel.
Because Cain kept on breathing
the smokesweet air
of another God, didn't he?
But Abel prays to me.

I was going to call this *necrophilia*

I was going to tell you about the dead baby that I held today, but I can't
tell you about the small not-life, light as fishbones, heavy as an anchor without a ship, something no doubt adrift without it. Shrunken by my perception of its lost-ness.

But I can't
tell you about the way the family mourned, the language created at Babel that everyone still understands, especially when something in the world is struck down by Heaven.

But I can't
tell you about the way I felt lost years dripping through my fingers, potential inking my hands in a holy, heart-bitter tattoo. A memory of the future, detached from a source of reference.

But I can't tell you.
Because death is a secret
picked out in all of our bones
with a shameful sickle silver needle
and whisper-black thread
that the world says
we should hide.

I can't tell you
how I shuffled past the baby bird's body the first time, hunched behind my coat, trying to forget that sparrows are more monogamous than people, and mourn like Mary Magdalene.

I can't tell you
how I looked both ways like an arsonist who sees an old wooden mansion, testing my religion of unlit matches, before retracing my steps and committing a new sin. Down like smoke.

I can't tell you
how the feathers felt against my palms, soft as baby-kisses, new as the plucked stems of spring grass I used to suck between my teeth until they were a vacuum of self.

But society won't let me tell you.
Because we mourn death
like we burn bridges
with crystal flames
that leave neither smoke
nor scent, because death is a
scarlet "A" sewing out lips shut.

Society won't let me tell you
that I cradled that body in the kindest way I know now, singing my primordial directive to protect the young and the gone. My hands were a gentle mausoleum, a kinetic apology.

Society won't let me tell you
that I gave the cold body some warmth like Prometheus
stealing fire from the gods to give it to the cold people, the
corpse people. I kindled hea as a kind of fleeting goodbye.

Society won't let me tell you
that I straightened pinions and quills still asleep in their
sheaths, baby-feathers poking out like daffodils, and carried
the body from the sidewalk to a quieter grave haunted by irises.

I was going to tell you about the dead baby sparrow that I held
   today,
but instead I'm standing oin front of a sink, hovering, staring
   with
glazed eyes as the water runs, as the soap accuses me of
dirtiness, as the mirror glares and says not to spread
my disease, my second-hand death. Still feeling
stiff, clawed feet clutching my fingers like
rings, I turn off the water. I smear
blasphemous hands over
everything I can
reach.

The Four Beasts of Tribulation

1. Afflicted with ravens,
thoughts the color of bleached bone.
Each breath has a snowdrift
between it.

2. A luna moth with no mouth
for any hunger. Time is condensed
and fractured, heaving and dropping free
like a full-bellied ship
into some deep Charybdis.

3. I used to be afraid
of water on both sides,
because it made me a bridge
over troubled water.
But now my body is the coelacanth
and my heart dreams
of bleeding.

4. Be the woman who
after a trauma
sits on the riverbank
feeding chicken thighs to crocodiles, mud
spilling through her sandals
and slick-coating old wounds.

We Skin Ourselves Daily

Without red teeth,
how can we talk
about such soul-baring things
as the pain we find
ourselves in, or
the happiness we swallow
in front of company
but never digest?
--
How can we talk
about the inner workings
of bone and body, where
the brain has no sway, where speaking
alone is a little like
skinning oneself before others.
Of course we're going

Field Notes on the Splinterbone Tree

Often mistaken for deadwood
bleached-bone stalk
a skinned body deceased limb
naked branches devoid of color or bark

Bleeds tiny red berries
not dangled at the tips of the branches like beckoning bells
clutched at the junctures of branches like secrets
knowing creatures of this world fight
harder for what is hidden than what is given

Body rooted in sepulcherous loam   decomposer
hearts-blood drops
Earth is littered with dead birds
the tree is eating them

Dear Phoenix

Stars love nothing but themselves,
There cold bright eyes
from cold, high shelves.

But you probably know that already,
like you know the bitter ash and brittle-dark sky.

I dreamt you stumbled like a wolf after a long winter, but
winter isn't gone yet, and your human-paws slid on snow
and slap-sharp ice, red chrysanthemums bleeding beneath
your heels; the kisses of a doomed Persephone.

I dreamt you left heat and soot in your wake, a bonfire's
breath that rose and let the stars breathe you in, slow and
heady; the night didn't exhale, didn't recognize the pillar
of fire you'd left behind, the pyre you'd leapt screaming from.

I dreamt you were a phoenix,
burning yourself to life.

I dreamt I could hear the hunt behind you, like God's
ethereal voice commanding *Get back on that cross where you
belong*, and you panicked from sole to soul, and the snow
thawed away from your every step like you were still afire.

I dreamt about your son, the boy with the cobalt eyes and fox-fire smile who lights a room on fire without anyone really knowing it, or questioning whether they should snuff him out, who kisses choir-boys on the mouth when society's glower is burning fields elsewhere.

Today's blasphemy child,
pretty and wild.

I dreamt that the moon kissed one of her eyes the color of cognac, the night sky the other, reflecting your cobalt fear that the devil really did give you those eyes and that the church should have burnt it all out of you, for all the stars to see.

I dreamt about your daughter, the girl with cognac eyes wreathed in the smoke of eyeliner, who can sing with the angels, but society paints her like the devil, saying that too much make-up hides the soul. She sings like you screamed at the stake:

pretty and wild
burnt and different.

I dreamt how you trembled, how you swallowed the word *witch,* and with you I tasted charcoal, the kingly salt of tears, and the crushed flowers turned sour in my mouth.
I've never tasted anything so blasphemous, so fine, so unforgettably force-fed.

I dreamt that you became Echidna, the one who birthed all the
so-called monsters of the world; the bastards, the defiers,
the questioners, the we-don't-fit-in-your-square-holes because
we're different and made of razors.

I dreamt your varicolored eyes,
past from antiquity to now.

When will the world learn?
We create witches
from the innocents we burn.

But you probably knew that already.

Chiaroscuro of Your Dark

I traverse the lonely places,
the spaces between your words,
where you pause for breath before

you find the path onwards,
words for shoes on your feet while I
shadow your tread-marks.

I'm the chiaroscuro of your dark
lashes above your pale skin,
casting shade when you blink, slow

as butterflies on the moon. I walk,
head down, hands in pockets,
in that barren gap between thought

and speech; I build the scarf
about my neck with the ideas
that never survive the journey.

It suffocates me and I revel in the
smothering. That emptiness you
feel where your ring sits too loose

and won't hug your skin,
where your skin doesn't fit
and won't kiss your bones,

I shuffle forward and drag
my untied shoelaces through
the hollow in your chest.

Pain is an echo you hear
only in hindsight, but it sticks
to my feet like ink when I toe

my sneakers off at your doormat.
I try not to track it in, but I'm made
for the lonely places, and I don't

know how to come in from the cold
without the cold coming in with me.
Without coloring the full with the empty.

No one

invites me to sink into the razor-dark,
to play the unstrung-harp we call a soul,
or to press lips the color of pomegranate seeds
up against the chill, unforgiving winter earth.
Just as no one invites winter to slip her
silky coat over the whole of the land, her slippers
a herald of stillness. Most days we have only
our inky body to move mountains with,
but it is our mountain and our body, and no one
invites us to challenge the lonely cold
with the live kiln hunger of our hearts.

Any Winter

There is this urge as I perch on my porch and tip my frown towards the stubborn, root-bound rose, the trailing vine, the valiant weed, looking at me like blithe dryads with their peridot eyes and periwinkle smiles. There is this urge to bring them all inside before Winter can get her claws on them. I feel like a greedy god who will not share. An amnesiac, stupid god, who forgets year after year that plants love the earth first and me a far distant second, even though I'd never set loose Winter's gasp on them, never crush the heads upon my lap with fists of frost. But I'm a heart-sore god who dies a little in the most pathetic way when I see all the earth's green things bending their heads to the bitter, biting chill, their supplicant hands rimed with frost while I'm warm and toasty inside, all of Summer's spoils at my altar. Surely I have room for them all? Surely my current fussy, root-bound nestlings – my haughty, secretive orchids whose flowers I've forgotten the colors of; my African Violets with their velveteen lips and persnickety hearts; that plant I lost the name of, but who grows uproariously as a testament to my mothering anyway – wouldn't mind just a bit more chlorochrous company? Another refugee from Winter or two? It would only be for the winter, I tell myself. Only for the winter, until they love me first, until the warmth of my hearth can sink into their roots, until they live on my exhale, bloom when I inhale. I'm like a cat closing its paws and sinking its sickle claws into soft feathers, and saying, *I'll only only love you so hard.*

Spring

Dayspell

Mirrors are a kind of exorcism
where I'm seeing something
that I've removed from that which I call
self, cuckolding the *other*
and building a long-ship for it
that I might cast out
upon the pewter waters
and light with ghastly fires
that I know will drown. The reflective surface
holds my face in chill, impersonal hands
and lets me lay down parts of my body
that don't easily attach to my
sense of myself. I was told
once that all mirrors were blank
in the beginning, and I wonder if
some day we will fill up all the mirrors
with exiles of our selves and call it
a new day.

Honey for Bones

Today I tried to control the commodification of my body.
I traded my floating ribs for the clean shears of a coelacanth
skull, because no matter what, the body won't protect those
littlest ribs; even God told Adam to trade them away.
Even the body-builder is vulnerable there, tucked behind the
hard pyramid of the elbow. I traded the birthmark on my
hand for my umbilical cord, because I lost it and feel that
I need it back, so that I can tie it to a horse's tale, fated to
leave me again but now to fall in some snowy winter pasture.
Tomorrow I plan to gather my past sad day – to bundle them
all up, pack them together in my hands, and coat them in
honey to make them more palatable to – and trade them for
a purr so deep the window rattles when I exhale.

Brave

Maybe someday I will take my
five-foot-nothing-with-my-hands-in-the-air
body and unfold it into something
petalled and steeled so that I can be—

one atlas moth surviving
even though she has no mouth
and she knows that beauty can't sustain anything, yet still she is—

a green knife of a body woven slowly
through the air, living off all the adventures
she survived when she was small, and didn't know the word—

Asexuality

You kiss me and your hands ask
> *can you love me*

And I answer
> squeezing the flesh around a mole on my left hand
> and thinking how it looks like a nipple   now you
> look at me and wonder *which mole is the nipple* like
> I wonder *which emotion is lust*

Your ten-seconds-too-long hugs ask
> *can you love me*

And I answer
> looking into the fridge and finding nothing good, no
> appetite meaning nobody looks good to me   you say
> *damn I'd fuck that* and I say *I'd snuggle with that like a
> sweater and share popcorn at most*

Your hands dimpling my hips ask
> *can you love me*

And I answer
> all the advertisements on television make no sense why
> does my hamburger come with plush lips   my life
> insurance with a headless body with breasts *who even is she*

You think about me late at night and your sighs ask
> *can you love me*

And I answer
>   a dove-grey sleeve with my arm pushing down it
>   like a throat, no bra meaning *I'm staying in tonight*
>   inside myself soul like a wool sock pleasure like a sieve

Your compliments on my figure ask
>   *can you love me*

And I answer
>   an unheeding body that wants things without a name
>   *frustrated as hell* but none of god's beings look good,
>   no body to cuddle up in   a gay man in a land of women

You sidle close and your body asks
>   *can you love me*

And I answer
>   an explanation repeated a million times in the silence
>   beneath my tongue *I hear if you cross your eyes too
>   long they'll stay that way rolled inward*   if I hold my
>   sexuality just-so will it stay that way

Your empty bed and naked warmth asks
>   *can you love me*

And I answer
>   a siren-song to the deaf *why is my crew swanning
>   overboard* a barracuda boy batting his eyes at me a
>   language I don't speak I look inside his teeth and
>   marvel at how he ever finds completion that way

Your thoughts of children with my eyes your smile ask
> *can you love me*

And I answer
> I can only give you *so much* of what you want you
> you at the top of love like it's a set of stairs to mount,
> looking down, asking *are you sad?* to where I sit on
> the lowest steps   and smile

You ask me
> *can you love me*

And I answer
> *come back when you know me by my name.*

Request of a Tsunami

Clean-slate-maker, show me the wet scrape
of your momentum, a vast, rasping tongue
of a blue tiger striped with white and thrashed
sea-floor until I don't remember what
a cluttered mind is. Show me how you can find renewal
with a seafloor upended, tossed
within the powerful tabernacle
of your cobalt, basalt, tumult body. You're more
stone-fist than you are water, only as weak
as the crack in the world-skin that birthed you,
tectonic plates as butterfly wings, it's ripple
reshaping entire swathes of shoreline.
Clean-slate-maker, give me a word for *forgiveness*
that is only for myself, forgiveness
that doesn't touch the abuser, forgiveness
that says *You don't owe the world*
a quite sea; calms only come after
you accept that there was a storm.

After five years of nurture and heartache, the Hoya bloomed

The sighing noise of dry dirt
expanding around rain
like a throat. My satisfaction
was a buzzard, featherless

head lubricated with blood and slipped
inside the carcass of lunch.
Cherish the guts first;
abandon the ugly. The smooth

granite curve
of the knee of *David*—
worn smooth by more hands
than Michelangelo—

begged for more. I wrapped
my satisfaction up in banana leaves,
placed it upon the coals to bury
and smoke it in the closed womb

of the earth and rot.
It tasted like coral, the salt
and the sea cut and scraped
deep into my tongue, licked out

between my fingers. Hoya blooms
like starfish peaking out
past fleshy leaves, smell so sweet
it makes your back-teeth ache.

The Happiness of the Poet

Happiness is
three orchids growing fat with blooms
proof that I can nurture something
well enough for it to burn

with color and light   happiness is
smoothing wire across the floor
and cutting it to length
fitting it with glue and cloth

for wings move loving than Icarus'
happiness is dipping a net
into a tank of pet shrimp and knowing
that they have never known fear

as they climb onto the mesh and touch
it with the tiny brushes of their hands
happiness is seven words scrawled
in permanent marker across my palm

I can only be patient and nurture

Prayers to the Maternal Mover

1. Esperinos

Ashen mother,
maker of all things grey and
sooted, make me an untouched coal
bursting upon your breath. I'll cinder my way
through all of the world and dream
of unbroken brittle things.

2. Apodipnon

Bitter mother,
goddess of blood and unhewn things,
mold me into a bezoar, abandon
the ugly into the palm of your hand until
there's but a crushed godstone
of me left behind.
Forgive me for the poisons I cannot cleanse
from your cup.

3. Mesonyktikon

Gaunt mother,
ruler of an angry child, make me
a Hoatzin bird that though I may be clawed
—hand and foot—in my youth
I'll grow more downy and feathered
and crowned with age.

4. Orthros

Whiskey mother,
ruler from a lowly place, let me
be your daughter-hound, a beast
that bites and burns and can only be tamed
with fire, burning off the alcohol of me.

5. Proti Ora

Shadowless mother,
space between a tiger's stripes,
make me a golden cage that I may hold
all of my guilt inside gilt
—like a heart inside ribs—
until even the fissures are holy.

6. Triti Ora

Ugly mother,
Butterfly-maker, make me a *vanda* orchid
with my face all purple and my veins
splayed. I'll forbear
the dirt of the earth
for you, for the naked air.

7. Ekti Ora

War mother,
maker and breaker within one body,
make me a bagpipe's scream
so that I won't be welcome
in any holy place but yours.
I'll howl across all the wide open places
until even the old bones shiver.

8. Enati Ora

Breathless mother,
weight of three rivers, make me barracuda dangerous,
a bird of prey beneath whatever water
drowns me. Lend me the strength
of five oceans and
the brutal blue.

Chats in a Rain Garden

the rain that falls behind
is a body to be grounded in   it wants
to make each raindrop a root   *come*

sit beside me
says the digitalis
with the spots down her throat

poison from tongue to lung
into all the night-blooming
flowers trapped in one mouth

runnels of rain down silver squill
like dim stars safe-harbored   like angels
that are buried in the gullets of oceans

and the thimbles of hummingbird nests
so deep you can barely say   *come*
drink beneath feathers and feet

The Greatest Smile

Today I'm so happy that I
could hold your hands
and dance
like binary planets
that nothing can stop
in their uproarious revolution.
And I don't even know you.

I know this elation
cannot last
but I plan to sew it
all up
in my heart with adamantine thread
where I can pluck it like lyre-strings
when I forget
what pitch the song of gladness is played in.

Today I'm so happy that I
would burst
into song
if I thought my mouth
could form the overflowing, supernova delight
that my heart so effortlessly sings.
And I'm usually tone-deaf.

My fingers
are
clumsy when
I'm miserable.
I might not find the thread
or strum it well.
But we cannot plan for rainy days
while the sky is pouring.
We must shake the motes
of sad
sorry dust
off our umbrellas while the sun
smiles.

Boy, when you're outside during a milk moon

don't think of her geisha face
or the lunar curve of misdirected
sun she gentles for you,
think of the Cyclops strength
of her one eye, a warrior more
focused for the loss of superfluous
dual vision, think of pockmarks
on an unblinking iris above you.
She's a breast lost
to cancer, a mass of scar-tissue
that makes shooting a bow easier.

Boy, don't think of how she
brightens the dark for you
because it's not for you, it's for
the 1.1 million pounds of thunderheads
ranked before her, it's for a dismantling
of daylight, it's for the fog that comes
ninety days before a rainstorm,
before the night-blooming cereus, all pulse
and petals suckled on night, before
the monolithic gasp
of dethroning a star, and the star
isn't even you.

Virago

You're expected to take your first step
like a sword leaping out of its scabbard, only a blade
has a sheath to cradle it home
while you're told, day one,
that you're just a hole for someone else
to sink into, a well
that others can always draw from. The world
says, you're a birthplace of the earth
but since you've got no flagpole
between your legs, you can't lay claim
to your own soil. You've got a hollowness
in you instead that's only valuable when filled.
So I say, fill it with an elephant heart,
not because its big or giving,
but because it seeks out the bones
of things and because it's shameless
in its home of wrinkles.
If you've got to be a font
of water for all to lap at,
then also build in you a hunger-stone
so that when the rivers eventually
run dry, you're not left with nothing,
you're left with a hard egg of yourself,
all alabaster and lined marble,
with words scored into it,
Wenn du mich siehst, dann weine:
If you see me, weep.

The New Sacrament

One tiny crush of coral
no small than a pea, no larger than
what you can hold pinched in the soft press
of your lips, pursed to inhale, just enough
to remind you that coral grows faster
when it is snapped and broken off,
but only because the broken pieces know each other,
each battered shard growing on its own
until it recognizes another splintered soulmate
and they grow stronger by knowing
one another to the core
Eat this, in remembrance of being whole

One smear of amber honey
atop of finger tipped already
in the pollen dust of a bumblebee's wing,
no more than you can stomach
when wracked by anxiety and a man-made
guilt – just enough that you can feel
the worker-bees fuzzy body
rubbed against your tongue and recall
that all the survival of the plants
rest upon her humble bumbling,
and that she can cook wasps to death
with the help of her sisters and her own heat.
Drink this, in remembrance of your own strength.

Mirror

I feel as though
if I could just lean into it
I'd fold and unfold like
a fractal, and reappear
on the other side of myself—
the *before* of myself—
and through the looking glass
hidden beneath my breastbone
maybe I'd see my mind
exhale itself slate-clean
like clouds scudding across
an eggshell sky.

Sing, sing, *cursor mundi*

Ring out
with drums for the lives
of saints, for the voices
of doves with the heads of trumpets.
Ring out with the cry
of the lute, the lyre,
the Castrati, the sinned upon
saint on the Katherine wheel
with all her broken ones and turns of fate.
Shrill the air
with old words, with Latin, with
Doelum non solum — Heaven, not earth — with
Dum spiro spero — while I breathe
I hope— until your voice grows hoarse, and God
feeds the ravens — *Deus pascit corus.*
Move your lungs
through the raucous founding
of the round table, move through,
move through, a throat
that bursts hellebore and holly
and thorned crowns, a voice
that *Bi þe se brinke No water þe nadrinke*
at the brink
of the sea let no waters drown thee.
Ruler of the world
I have endured the silence,
let the creation begin.

Happiness in Green

Today I bury my hands in earth up to my elbows, and tickle the world's toes as dirt mingles with my nail polish. Today I marvel at new orchid roots revealed pale and fresh as a baby's hands or a scar – a whiter, cleaner seam than the skin you'd lost to violence. Today I put the roots back into the pot, let her grasp at the bark and moss with renewed vigor, and imagine my childhood self playing in the world with unsullied hands. Today I stay gloriously quiet and ponder the praying mantis hunkered on my wrist, scooped carefully just now from my coatrack where he thought he might catch flies. He angles his head at me, as if he can hear the singing beneath my skin. He holds with polite chitinous claws to the fine hairs of my arm, and I revel in my ability to be gentle. Today I know that I have not hurt a creature less powerful than me. Today I practice a tenderness as pure as a bone-deep choir, the lyrics sent along the lines of my fingers to touch the living in the smallest ways. Tomorrow may sew sorrows in my blood, but today I dig my own roots deeper, and trust that orchids need no dirt and mantises shed their skins like second-best dresses discarded before a midnight run through moon-backed grasses.

Prayer for a Long Union

Let me be your longest shadow,
let me be your darkest night,
Let me be your armed right hand
let me be your wrought iron bite.

Let me be the sand you crash on,
let me be the be the space you fill.
Let me be the reddest nightmare
of all who wish you ill.

Let the winter crack the marrow
and the summer scorch the earth,
but let the strength of our twinned hands
never know lack or dearth.

So let me build a boat with flexing sides
which knows a North that is true,
that I may thrive in a gentle earthquake
whose epicenter is you.

Daughtermoth, become a queen

but not a dung beetle
be a morpho, a blue
bloom
birdeater
full of cairns and birdwings
and nectar.
Inside your meadowlark,
metalmark
skin grow a hive
and fill it with tethered dreams
so that when the moon rises,
you'll be twenty
dune scorpions at night,
a luna moth, a lady-
bird spider, a death's-
head crown of
xerxes blues,
all extinct
to men's hands.

Maia Carlson is a Canadian transplant living in Kansas since 1997, whose Bachelors degree in biology somehow led to a Masters in English in 2018. Her interest in poetry is recent, although she's now published in *Rogue Agent, Touchstone, the Burmingham Poetry Review,* and a few others. As an asexual-aromantic poet, she enjoys exploring atypical forms of connection in her poetry, all while interweaving her past studies in biology. She now teaches persuasive and technical writing to college students at Kansas State University as a term instructor.

www.ingramcontent.com/pod-product-compliance
Lightning Source LLC
Chambersburg PA
CBHW030121100526
44591CB00009B/478